Tools

Search

Notes

Discuss

MyReportLinks.com Books

Go!

TOP TEN COUNTRIES OF RECENT IMMIGRANTS

SOUTH KOREA

A MyReportLinks.com Book

South Huntington Pub. Lib.
145 Pidgeon Hill Rd.
Huntington Sta., N.Y. 11746

Lisa Harkrader

MyReportLinks.com Books

an imprint of
Enslow Publishers, Inc.
Box 398, 40 Industrial Road
Berkeley Heights, NJ 07922
USA

915.19
Harkrader

MyReportLinks.com Books, an imprint of Enslow Publishers, Inc. MyReportLinks® is a registered trademark of Enslow Publishers, Inc.

Copyright © 2004 by Enslow Publishers, Inc.

All rights reserved.

No part of this book may be reproduced by any means without the written permission of the publisher.

Library of Congress Cataloging-in-Publication Data

Harkrader, Lisa.
  South Korea / Lisa Harkrader.
    v. cm. — (Top ten countries of recent immigrants)
  Includes index.
  Contents: Korea: land of the morning calm — Land and climate — Culture — Economy — History — Korean Americans.
  ISBN 0-7660-5181-1 (alk. paper)
  1. Korea (South)— Juvenile literature. 2. Korean Americans—Juvenile literature. [1. Korea (South) 2. Korean Americans.] I. Title. II. Series.
  DS907.4.H37 2004
  951.95—dc22
                            2003023318

Printed in the United States of America

10 9 8 7 6 5 4 3 2 1

To Our Readers:
Through the purchase of this book, you and your library gain access to the Report Links that specifically back up this book.
The Publisher will provide access to the Report Links that back up this book and will keep these Report Links up to date on **www.myreportlinks.com** for three years from the book's first publication date.
We have done our best to make sure all Internet addresses in this book were active and appropriate when we went to press. However, the author and the Publisher have no control over, and assume no liability for, the material available on those Internet sites or on other Web sites they may link to.
The usage of the MyReportLinks.com Books Web site is subject to the terms and conditions stated on the Usage Policy Statement on **www.myreportlinks.com**.
A password may be required to access the Report Links that back up this book. The password is found on the bottom of page 4 of this book.
Any comments or suggestions can be sent by e-mail to comments@myreportlinks.com or to the address on the back cover.

Photo Credits: © Corel Corporation, pp. 1, 10, 16, 29, 30; Artville, p. 3; Asia Society, p. 20; BBC, p. 12; Enslow Publishers, Inc., p. 15; Guggenheim Museum, p. 44; *Honolulu Star-Bulletin*, p. 42; Library of Congress, pp. 25, 35, 38; Metropolitan Museum of Art, pp. 23, 33; MyReportLinks.com Books, pp. 4, back cover; PBS, pp. 21, 37; Photos.com, p. 1; The Department of Defense Visual Information Service/National Archives and Records Administration, p. 27; The Nobel Foundation, p. 39; *The World Factbook 2003* pp. 1, 9 (flags).

Cover Photos: Flags, *The World Factbook 2003*; Kids, Photos.com; Royal Tombs, Kyongju, © Corel Corporation.

Contents

    Report Links 4

    South Korea Facts 9

1 **Korea: Land of the Morning Calm** 10

2 **Land and Climate** 14

3 **Culture** 19

4 **Economy** 27

5 **History** 32

6 **Korean Americans** 41

    Chapter Notes 46

    Further Reading 47

    Index 48

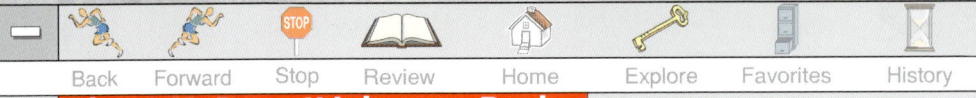

About MyReportLinks.com Books

MyReportLinks.com Books
Great Books, Great Links, Great for Research!

The Report Links listed on the following four pages can save you hours of research time by **instantly** bringing you to the best Web sites relating to your report topic.

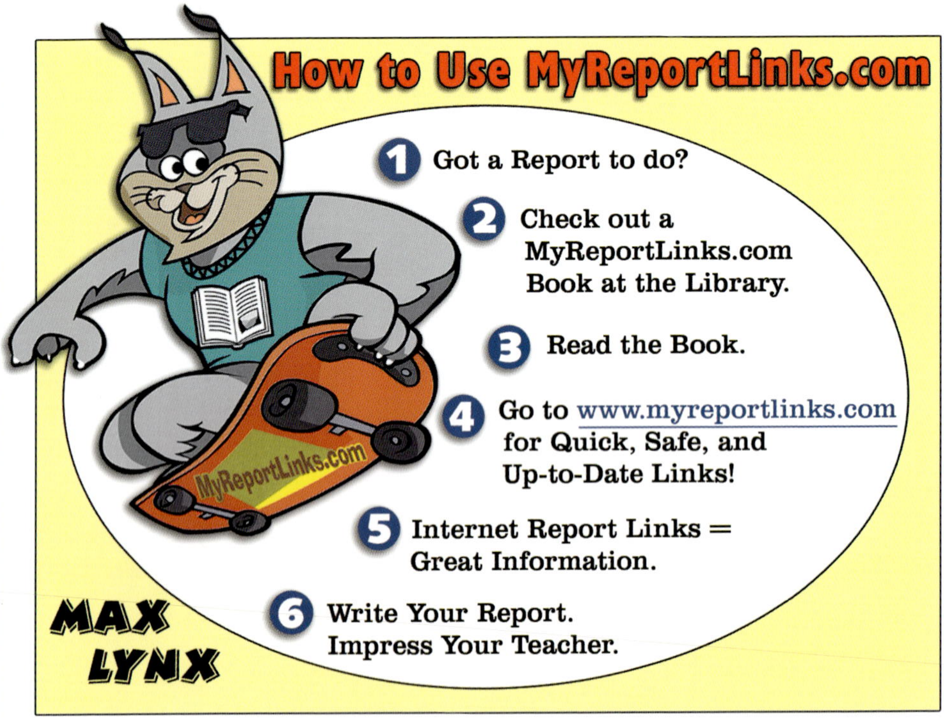

How to Use MyReportLinks.com

1. Got a Report to do?
2. Check out a MyReportLinks.com Book at the Library.
3. Read the Book.
4. Go to www.myreportlinks.com for Quick, Safe, and Up-to-Date Links!
5. Internet Report Links = Great Information.
6. Write Your Report. Impress Your Teacher.

MAX LYNX

The pre-evaluated Web sites are your links to source documents, photographs, illustrations, and maps. They also provide links to dozens—even hundreds—of Web sites about your report subject.

MyReportLinks.com Books and the MyReportLinks.com Web site save you time and make report writing easier than ever!

Please see "To Our Readers" on the copyright page for important information about this book, the MyReportLinks.com Web site, and the Report Links that back up this book. Please enter **ISK4481** if asked for a password.

   MyReportLinks.com Books

Tools   Search   Notes   Discuss

Report Links

Go!

 The Internet sites described below can be accessed at http://www.myreportlinks.com

Editor's Choice

▶ **The *World Factbook*: Korea, South**
This page from the *World Factbook* contains statistics about South Korea. Geography, people, government, economy, communications, transportation, military, and transnational issues are covered here.

Editor's Choice

▶ **South Korea—A Country Study**
This Library of Congress site contains a comprehensive study of South Korea, including its history, geography, and culture.

Editor's Choice

▶ **BBC: The Korean War In Depth**
This BBC feature contains a history of the Korean War. Here you will find photographs, sound clips, and related articles to help put the war into perspective.

Editor's Choice

▶ **One Hundred Years of Korean Immigration to the United States**
This page from the United States Embassy to South Korea celebrates one hundred years of Korean immigration to America and provides links to Web sites about Korea and Korean Americans.

Editor's Choice

▶ **Learn About Korea**
On this Web site, you can learn about South Korea's people, geography, language, national symbols, history, and more.

Editor's Choice

▶ **Commanding Heights: South Korea**
This PBS site focuses on the South Korean economy. Historic, political, social, environmental, and legal factors are explored in depth.

Any comments? Contact us: comments@myreportlinks.com   5

Back　Forward　Stop　Review　Home　Explore　Favorites　History

Report Links

The Internet sites described below can be accessed at
http://www.myreportlinks.com

▶ **About Seoul: City Facts**
From the official Web site for the city of Seoul, South Korea, you will find information on this capital's history, economy, transportation, and more.

▶ **Arts of Korea**
This site from the Metropolitan Museum of Art provides the museum's Arts of Korea exhibition. Included are examples of Korean ceramics, metalwork, decorative arts, Buddhist sculpture, and painting.

▶ **AsiaInfo.org: South Korea**
This site contains articles, maps, photographs, and links related to South Korea's land, history, and culture.

▶ **AskAsia: Korea**
Here you will find a wide range of articles about Korea. History, geography, religion, society, government, arts, international relations, and many other topics are covered.

▶ **Conflict and Consequence: The Korean War and Its Unsettled Legacy**
This Korean War exhibit from the Truman Presidential Museum and Library contains articles, documents, photographs, and more on the conflict known as the Korean War.

▶ **The Embassy of Korea in the U.S.A.**
This Web site contains news and information about South Korea's political, economic, and military relations with the United States.

▶ **Hidden Korea**
This PBS site contains a brief introduction to South Korea. Geography, history, culture, religion, and food are discussed here.

▶ **Honolulu Star Bulletin: A Better Life**
This Hawaiian newspaper article takes a look at one hundred years of Korean immigration to the islands and includes interviews with Korean Americans.

Any comments? Contact us: comments@myreportlinks.com

 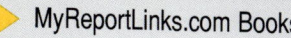

Tools   Search   Notes   Discuss

Report Links

 The Internet sites described below can be accessed at
http://www.myreportlinks.com

▶The International Tae Kwon Do Association
This Web site of the International Tae Kwon Do Association offers background on the Korean martial art, including its philosophy, a history of its founder, and translations of Korean terms used in tae kwon do.

▶Korean Cultural Center: About Korea
This site from the Los Angeles Korean Cultural Center contains a wealth of information about Korea. Here you will learn about Korean language, arts, lifestyle, heritage, tourism, food, and more.

▶Korean History Project
The Korean History Project provides an in-depth look into Korea's past. Inside you will find an interactive time line, essays, and more.

▶Korean War Veterans Memorial
The official National Park Service site of Washington's Korean War Veterans Memorial contains facts about Korean history, the Korean War, and the monument itself.

▶Koreatown Monument and Pocket Park
This site presents a brief description and illustrations of a monument to be completed in 2004 that will serve as a gateway to Koreatown, the Korean-American community in Los Angeles. The monument replicates a historic Korean pavilion.

▶Life in Korea: Cultural Spotlight
This site contains a number of in-depth feature articles about topics as varied as the Demilitarized Zone and tae kwon do.

▶Linda Sue Park
At the official site of poet and children's author Linda Sue Park, you will find information about her life, books, and more.

▶New York Philharmonic: Sarah Chang
Korean-American Sarah Chang is one of the most popular classical violinists in the world. Her New York Philharmonic site contains her biography, an interview, and information about upcoming performances.

Any comments? Contact us: comments@myreportlinks.com   7

Report Links

The Internet sites described below can be accessed at http://www.myreportlinks.com

▶ The Nobel Peace Prize 2000: Kim Dae-jung
Former South Korean president Kim Dae-jung won the Nobel Peace Prize in 2000 for his peaceful policies towards North Korea. Here you will find a brief biography, the text of his acceptance speech, and other resources.

▶ North Korea—A Country Study
This Library of Congress Web site contains a comprehensive study of North Korea, including its history, geography, and culture.

▶ North Korea Nuclear Standoff: The Demilitarized Zone
The Demilitarized Zone, or DMZ, marks the heavily fortified border between North Korea and South Korea. Here you will learn about the zone, its history, and its importance.

▶ Office of the President: Republic of Korea
This is the official site of South Korean president Roh Moo-hyun. Here you will learn about the current president and South Korea's government, history, culture, symbols, language, and more.

▶ Syngman Rhee
Syngman Rhee was elected the first president of South Korea in 1948. This CNN page contains a brief overview of his life and political career.

▶ Time Asia: Park Chung-hee
Park Chung-hee overthrew the existing South Korean government in 1961. He ruled the country for eighteen years. Here you will learn about Park's presidency and relationship with the United States.

▶ What Is Korean Buddhism?
This site focuses on the teachings and history of Korean Buddhism. It also features information about important Buddhist temples and life in Korean Buddhist monasteries.

▶ The Worlds of Nam June Paik
This site from the Guggenheim Museum celebrates the art and life of Nam June Paik, including a brief biography of the artist, a description of the exhibit, and some images of his most famous works.

Any comments? Contact us: comments@myreportlinks.com

South Korea Facts

▶ **Official Name**
Republic of Korea

▶ **Capital**
Seoul

▶ **Population**
48,289,037 (July 2003 estimate)[1]

▶ **Total Area**
38,023 square miles (98,480 square kilometers)[2]

▶ **Highest Point**
Halla-san, 6,398 feet (1,950 meters)[3]

▶ **Lowest Point**
Sea level

▶ **Location**
On the southern half of the Korean Peninsula on the eastern coast of Asia

▶ **Type of Government**
Republic

▶ **Head of State**
President

▶ **Monetary Unit**
Won

▶ **Language**
Korean

▶ **National Anthem**
Aegug-ga ("Patriotic Hymn")

▶ **Flag**
South Korea's flag is called the *Taegeuk-gi*. The flag's white background symbolizes light and purity and reflects the desire of the Korean people for peace and harmony. In the center is a red and blue *taegeuk*—yin and yang—that symbolizes complementary opposites of a universe in balance.

Four sets of black bars, called trigrams, surround the taeguek in each corner of the flag. The set of three solid bars represents heaven, spring, creativity, and generosity. The three broken bars represent earth, summer, and righteousness. The set of two solid bars and one broken bar stands for the sun, autumn, fire, loyalty, and courtesy. The set of two broken bars and one solid bar stands for the moon, winter, water, wisdom, and danger.

Chapter 1 ▶

Korea: Land of the Morning Calm

South Korea is a mountainous country on the southern half of the Korean peninsula. The Korean peninsula is a thumb of land that juts into the sea from northeastern Asia. For more than twelve hundred years, the peninsula was home to a unified Korea. The ancient Korean nation, however, fell victim to the policies of the Cold War and since 1945 has been split into two countries, North Korea and South Korea. That split has affected all Koreans ever since.

According to Korean folklore, Korea was founded in 2333 B.C. by the son of a bear-woman who united with a divine being. Legend says that a tiger and a bear both prayed

▲ *A Korean temple.*

to the Divine Creator to make them human. The Divine Creator's son, Hwanung, gave them each twenty pieces of garlic and a bitter herb called mugwort. He told them to eat the garlic and mugwort and live in a cave, out of the sun, for one hundred days. The tiger soon became restless and left. But the bear was patient and stayed in the cave. When the bear finally emerged after one hundred days, Hwanung turned it into a beautiful woman. Hwanung married the bear-woman, and they had a son named Tan'gun. According to the legend, Tan'gun was the first king of Korea.

Tan'gun was the founder of a dynasty that ruled northern Korea for hundreds of years. He called his kingdom *Chosun*, which means "land of the morning calm." The name refers to the early morning mists that cloak the forests and mountains of Korea. But throughout its long history, Korea has seen very little calm.

North and South

The Korean peninsula is located between the mainland of Asia and the islands of Japan a few hundred miles to the east. Koreans sometimes call their land the "shrimp between whales" because larger and more powerful neighbors have tried to control their homeland throughout history.[1]

In 1905, imperial Japan, one of those "whales," gained control of the Korean peninsula after defeating China and Russia in separate wars. In 1910, Japan annexed Korea and made it a colony, ending its long history as a unified state. Japan's harsh rule of Korea lasted for thirty-five years.

In 1945, the Allied countries, which included the United States, Great Britain, France, and the Soviet Union, defeated Japan in World War II and liberated Korea. Since there was no Korean government to take over the country, two of the Allied nations, the United States and the Soviet Union, took control of the peninsula. They

▲ *The Korean War began on June 25, 1950, when North Korea launched a surprise attack on South Korea.*

established what the United States expected would be a temporary dividing line along the 38th parallel. The Soviet Union controlled the northern half, and the United States controlled the southern half. The goal was to restore order. But by 1948, the Soviet Union had formed a Communist government to rule northern Korea. South Koreans established a democratic republic in the south. Since then, the ethnic Korean nation has been divided into two separate countries: the Republic of Korea, or South Korea, and the Democratic People's Republic of Korea, or North Korea. The hope of most South Koreans today is to make Korea a unified nation once again.

The DMZ

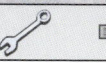

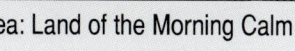

In 1950, North Korea invaded South Korea to reunify Korea by force. Led by the United States, many of the nations that were members of the United Nations sent troops to help South Korea as part of the United Nations Command. China then stepped in to help North Korea, with the Soviet Union also providing aid. The UN Command and the Communists fought each other for three long years in a bloody conflict known as the Korean War. In 1953, the two sides reached a truce that ended the fighting, but a peace agreement was never concluded.

The truce established a buffer zone that became the border between the two countries. This two-and-a-half-mile-wide (four-kilometer-wide) strip of land is called the Demilitarized Zone (DMZ). The DMZ is the most heavily armed border in the world. Nearly 2 million soldiers face off across this strip of land. North Korean troops guard the northern side, and South Korean and American troops defend the southern side. Tall, razor-wire fences and watchtowers line each side of the DMZ, which is booby-trapped with mines. When United States president Bill Clinton visited the DMZ in 1993, he called it "the scariest place on Earth."[2]

Nearly one quarter of all South Koreans have family members who live on the other side of the DMZ whom they have not been able to see for many years. Until mid-2000, South Koreans could not enter North Korea, and North Koreans could not leave. But in 1998, relations between North Korea and South Korea improved, and in 2000, the heads of the two countries met for the first time and agreed to make it easier for separated family members to see each other. Since then, thousands of Korean families have been reunited—if only for brief periods.

Chapter 2

Land and Climate

South Korea is bordered by North Korea in the north and three bodies of water to the west, east, and south. The Yellow Sea, or West Sea, lies to the west, separating South Korea from China. The Korea Strait lies to the south, and the Sea of Japan lies to the east. But you will never find the label *Sea of Japan* on a Korean map. Koreans insist that this sea should be called the East Sea, which is what it was called before Japan annexed Korea in 1910. The East Sea and the Korea Strait separate Korea from the islands of Japan.

▶ The Lay of the Land

When Koreans describe their country, they often say *san nomo san itta* ("over the mountains, more mountains").[1] Mountains cover 70 percent of South Korea. These mountains are not tall, but they are rugged. Steep ridges tower above deep valleys. Thick forests blanket the slopes. Rivers and streams flow from the mountains and cut across the peninsula.

The craggy Taebaek Mountains run along South Korea's east coast. These mountains push right up to the coastline and plunge into the East Sea. Smaller mountain ranges thrust through the center of the country. Over three thousand islands fringe South Korea's southern and western coasts. These islands are the tips of mountains jutting from the sea.

South Korea's tallest peak, Halla-san (6,398 feet; 1,950 meters), is an extinct volcano. It has not erupted since A.D. 1007. Its peak and slopes form South Korea's largest island, Cheju-do, which lies off the southern tip of

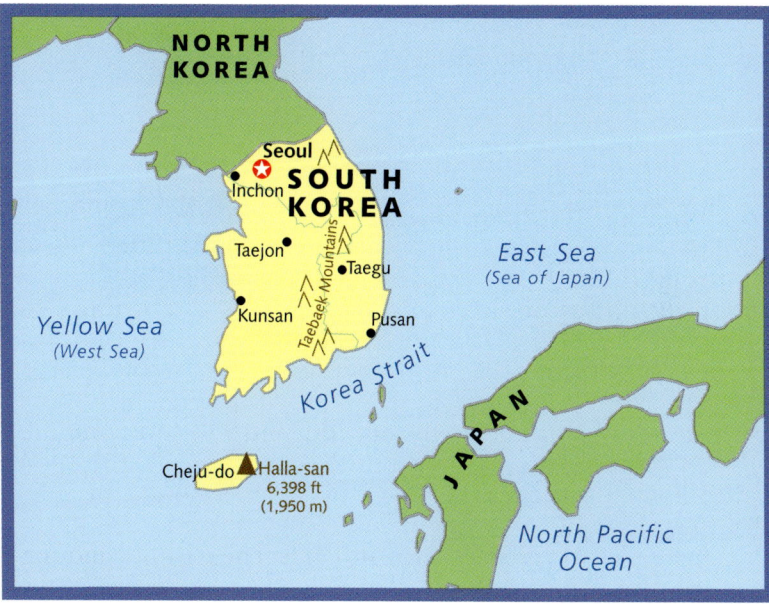

▲ A map of Korea.

the peninsula. Lava caves and tunnels pit Halla-san's slopes. Its volcanic crater fills with water and becomes a lake during the rainy summer months. Korea no longer has active volcanoes, but thermal activity deep underground creates hot springs. These springs bubble up throughout the country.

The mountains in central and eastern South Korea gradually give way to more gentle hills, plains, and river valleys along the southern and western coasts. Only about 20 percent of South Korea's land can be farmed. Most of the farmland lies in lowlands. Many of the country's largest cities, such as the capital, Seoul, also lie in the south and west.

The Yellow Sea, on the country's west coast, has one of the highest tides in the world. At Inchon, a port city on the Yellow Sea, the tide rises as much as 33 feet (9 meters).

Only the Bay of Fundy in Canada has a greater difference between high and low tides.

▶ The Four Seasons

South Korea lies in the temperate climate zone, like the upper mid-Atlantic region of the United States, and has four seasons: winter, spring, summer, and autumn. These seasons are shaped by strong winds that blow across the peninsula at different times of the year.

In winter, cold, dry winds sweep in from Siberia. Winter lasts from December to March and can be bitterly cold, especially in the north. Winter temperatures often fall into a pattern of three cold days followed by four warmer days.

Koreans have devised many ways to fend off winter's cold. For thousands of years, they have heated their homes with *ondol* floors. *Ondol* means "warm stone." Ondol floors are made of thick concrete or stone. Hot air or water runs through pipes in the concrete, heating the

▲ *South Korea's winter season is extremely cold with temperatures often falling below freezing.*

house. Many Koreans sit, eat, and sleep on the floor because it is so warm.

The peninsula begins thawing in April. In early spring, winds from the Asian mainland sometimes gust across the peninsula. These winds, called *hwangsa*, carry yellow dust from the Gobi Desert in Mongolia.

Korean summers are hot and wet. In late June, strong winds called monsoons begin blowing in from the Pacific Ocean, dumping heavy rain across the peninsula. About 70 percent of Korea's yearly rain falls during the summer. Korean farmers rely on the monsoons to water their crops. Rice farmers, especially, need the rains to soak their rice paddies. But too much rain can cause flooding. The government has dammed some of South Korea's rivers to control floods and produce electricity.

Late summer typhoons sometimes blast the Korean coast. Typhoons are tropical ocean cyclones that bring destructive winds, heavy rains, and violent ocean waves.

▶ Wildlife

Dense old-growth forests once covered Korea. Through the centuries, people cut trees for firewood and lumber. The Korean War, fought from 1950 to 1953, devastated Korea's forests. By war's end, the peninsula had become nearly bare. In the 1960s, the South Korean government imposed limits on cutting trees, began a tree-planting program, and established April 5 of each year as Arbor Day, a national holiday to plant trees. Since then, South Koreans have planted millions of trees. Today, new forests cover the country.

Flowers such as lotuses, lilacs, rhododendrons, and azaleas bloom across the country. The national flower is the *mugunghwa*, or rose of Sharon. South Koreans admire the rose of Sharon for its strength. When you cut a rose of

Sharon, it grows back, just as Korea has always grown back when other countries have tried to cut it down. South Korea's most famous and most prized plant is ginseng. Ginseng root is believed to bolster health and alertness. People all over the world use Korean ginseng in tea, food, medicine, and even candy.

Over 370 species of birds live in Korea for at least part of the year. Korean wetlands are a natural stopping place for birds migrating between northern Asia and areas in the southern Pacific and Australia. Two species of birds that live on the peninsula year-round are cranes and magpies. Magpies are the national bird of South Korea. Koreans consider both magpies and cranes to bring good luck.

South Korea is home to leopards, bears, wolves, lynx, deer, badgers, and wild boars. Unfortunately, many of these animals have become rare because people have moved into their habitats. People have also hunted these animals for their fur and for body parts, such as bear gall bladders and deer antlers, that are used in folk medicine. To protect these animals, the South Korean government has set restrictions on hunting.

The Demilitarized Zone (DMZ) may be a scary place for humans, but it has become a refuge for Korea's plants and animals. Without people to create pollution or destroy their habitats, many of Korea's rare and endangered species thrive here. For years, scientists believed that the Manchurian crane was extinct in Korea. But in the 1970s, they found a colony of these cranes living in the DMZ. Siberian tigers, a traditional symbol of Korea, once roamed the Korean peninsula. They were thought to have become nearly extinct, but recently, naturalists have found signs that these animals may also live in the DMZ. [2]

Chapter 3

Culture

With more than 48 million people living on less than forty thousand square miles, South Korea is one of the most densely populated countries on Earth. One quarter of all South Koreans live in Seoul, the country's capital and one of the world's largest cities.

▶ Courtesy, Clothing, Food, and Marriage

Koreans are very polite. One way they show politeness is by bowing, the way Americans might shake hands. When Koreans meet or say good-bye, they give each other a short bow. If they want to show a great deal of respect toward someone important, they bow more deeply.

Many South Koreans wear the same kinds of clothing that people in western countries wear. Some South Koreans still wear the traditional loose-fitting Korean *hanbok*, especially when celebrating a holiday or wedding. They eat traditional Korean foods, such as a spicy pickled cabbage dish called *kimchi*, but they also eat hamburgers, pizza, and other western-style foods. Matchmakers used to arrange marriages in South Korea, but most South Koreans now choose their own husbands or wives.

▶ Confucianism's Impact

The teachings of Confucius, an ancient Chinese philosopher who lived from about 551 to 479 B.C., still influence South Korean culture. Confucianism is a philosophy, or system of beliefs, that is concerned with behavior and social order. Confucius taught that a nation and its

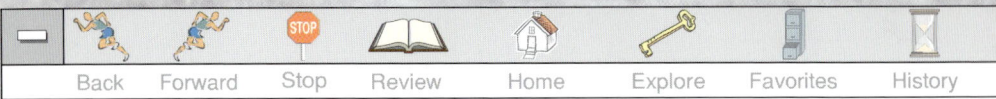

▲ Chinese cabbages were introduced in Korea during the nineteenth century. Kimchi was created when these cabbages were fermented with various spices, including hot red pepper, which gives the dish its red coloring.

people should function as members of a family for the greatest good. Five relationships, in particular, were the most important: that of father to eldest son, ruler to subjects, husband to wife, elder to younger brother, and friend to friend. In Confucian thought, it is important that younger people respect elders. Confucius believed that each person was born into a social class and that society functioned best when each person stayed in his or her own class. But he also believed that a person could achieve the highest class if he or she demonstrated exceptional skill and could pass written tests.

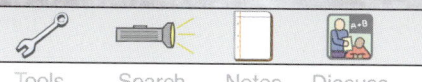

Confucian virtues—including courtesy, intelligence, honesty, justice, and honoring ancestors and elders—have shaped Korean culture. The Korean people are respectful. They believe studying hard will improve their lives. They center their lives around their families. But the influences of industrialization and western culture have weakened the influence of Confucianism in Korea and elsewhere.

▶ Religion in South Korea

South Koreans practice many different faiths, but the largest number, 49 percent, are Christians. Christian missionaries,

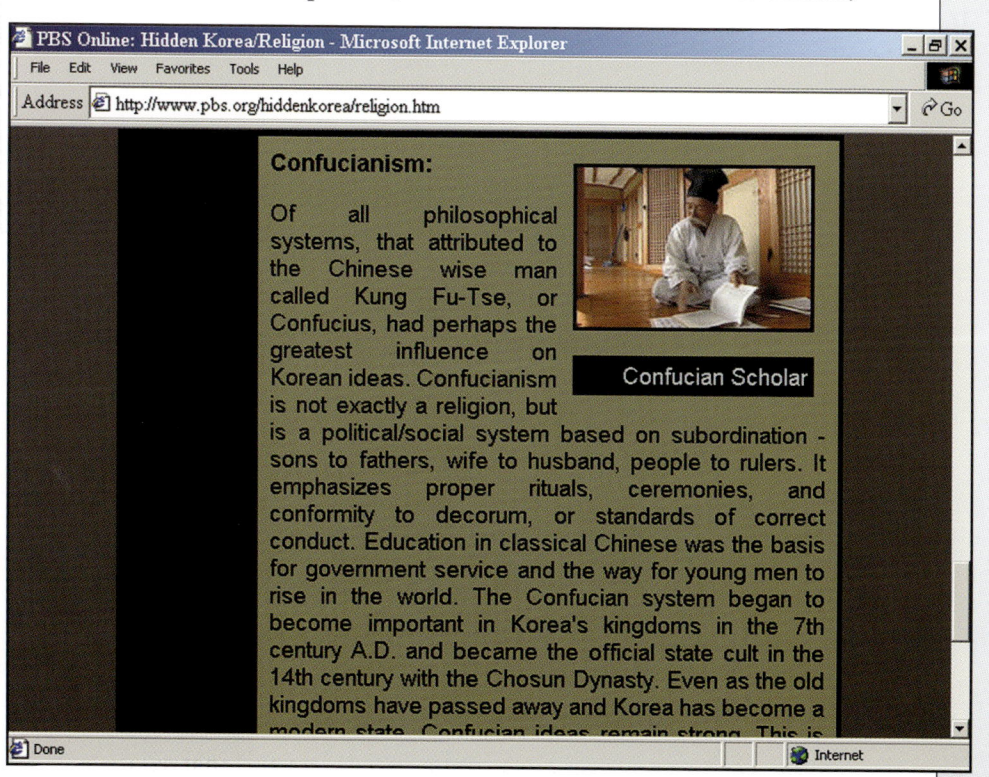

▲ Korean thought has probably been most influenced by the philosophy of Kung Fu-Tse, or Confucius. Confucianism rose to prominence in Korea in the seventh century.

21

who began entering Korea in 1794, had a great impact on the country. They established schools and hospitals and converted many Koreans to their religion.

About 47 percent of South Koreans are Buddhists. Buddhists follow the teachings of Buddha, a Hindu prince who lived in India from about 563 to 483 B.C. Buddhists do not pray to gods. They believe in looking within themselves for truth instead. Buddhists strive to do away with worldly wants and goods and seek their spiritual self.

A small number of South Koreans still practice an ancient religion called shamanism. They believe that spirits live in natural objects such as mountains or trees and that only a special priestess called a shaman, or *mudang*, can communicate with these spirits. The mudang contacts a spirit through a ritual called a *kut*. During the kut, she may sing, dance, and offer gifts to the spirit.

▸ Language

South Koreans speak Korean, a language related to Turkish, Finnish, Mongolian, and Japanese. The Korean language also contains many words borrowed from Chinese.

Until the fifteenth century, Koreans used Chinese characters to write their language. But Koreans found it difficult to express themselves using characters developed for another language. The Chinese written language contained thousands of characters. These characters took years to learn, and only the wealthiest Koreans could spend that much time studying. Most Koreans could not read or write.

In the 1400s, King Sejong, one of the greatest Korean rulers, decided that all Koreans should be able to read and write. He appointed a group of experts to develop an alphabet for the Korean language. That alphabet, invented

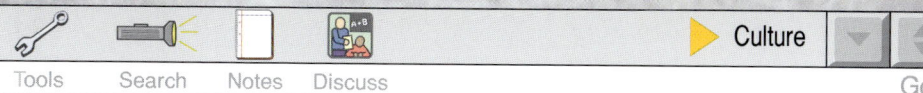

in 1444, is called *hangul*. Hangul is a phonetic alphabet. It has twenty-four letters that represent sounds spoken in the Korean language. Hangul is much less complicated than the Chinese system of characters. All Koreans, not just the educated upper classes, could easily learn hangul.

Each year, on October 9, South Koreans celebrate the invention of their alphabet on Hangul Day. South Korea has a high rate of literacy—approximately 98 percent of the adult population can read and write.[1]

▶ Family Names

Most Koreans have three names. Their family name, or surname, which Americans call a last name, comes first,

▲ This Buddha statue, the Buddha of Medicine, holds in its right hand a round object thought to represent healing.

23

followed by the given name. Many Korean Americans and Koreans who work closely with Americans will sometimes state their given name first and then their family name.

The given name, which has two parts, has traditionally depended on the child's gender (boy or girl) and generation. Parents traditionally name daughters with two names that have special meaning for them.

When naming sons, however, Koreans take one of the two given names and make it a third, or generation, name that brothers share. The other given name is unique to each son. Many South Korean families today are relatively small, and may not include sons, so South Korean parents have begun to choose names for their sons that do not follow the traditional requirements of generation names.

▶ Sports and Games

South Koreans enjoy many of the same sports that Americans enjoy, such as baseball, golf, Ping-Pong, basketball, and soccer. In 2002, South Korea and Japan hosted the FIFA World Cup, soccer's most important event. Koreans also play sports and games that are unique to their culture. Tae kwon do is a Korean martial art similar to karate. Tae kwon do originated in Korea over a thousand years ago and is one of the most popular sports in the country. *Ssirum,* an ancient Korean style of wrestling similar to Japanese sumo wrestling, is also popular. Another popular game is *Baduk,* also called *Go,* which is a board game in which players use black or white stones to capture as much territory as possible on a playing board made up of 324 small squares.

The seesaw is a traditionally popular game for Korean girls. A Korean seesaw is a wide plank balanced over a roll of straw. A girl seesaws standing up, jumping onto her end

▲ *In this archival photograph, two Korean men play Baduk.*

of the plank, then bounding high into the air as her partner lands on the other end. Centuries ago, Korean women were rarely allowed to leave their homes. It is believed that they began seesawing as a way to see over the high walls that surrounded their houses.

Today, most Korean boys and girls enjoy the same sports and also enjoy electronic toys and games as well as computers as much as children in western countries do.

▶ **Birthday Parties**

Birthdays are important milestones for Koreans. When a Korean child is one hundred days old, his family throws a special party called a *baek-il*. The custom began centuries ago, when many babies died before their hundredth day. Korean families continue the tradition even though most South Koreans can expect to live into their seventies.

On a Korean child's first birthday, called *tol*, his family throws another party. They place gifts in front of him, such

as thread, pencils, books, money, and arrows. Whatever gift the child chooses is said to predict his future. If he picks thread, he will live a long life. If he picks a pencil or book, he will do well in school. If he chooses money, he will be rich, and if he chooses an arrow, he will have a military career.

Koreans mark their sixtieth birthday, *hwangap*, with another big celebration. According to the Korean zodiac, sixty years completes one life cycle. So someone who has lived sixty years is a very honored person. At the hwangap celebration, family members show their respect in a formal bowing ceremony called *kun chul*.

▶ Over There

Most South Koreans share the same history, customs, and language. The exception is Cheju-do. Over the centuries, this island, separated from the peninsula by over 50 miles (80 kilometers) of water, developed a culture different from the rest of Korea.

Cheju translates as "the district over there." In the 1200s, Mongols invaded and ruled Cheju-do for a hundred years. They influenced the clothing, customs, and language of the island. Today, islanders speak a dialect of Korean that is slightly different from the language spoken by Koreans on the peninsula. The Mongols also brought horses, and Cheju-do became an important horse-breeding center.

Cheju-do is a volcanic island. Scattered across Cheju-do are large harabang, or grandfather stones, carved from lava rocks. These ancient sculptures feature bulging eyes and skinny arms. Experts are not sure who created the harabang or why they were created, but for centuries the harabang have been a symbol of the island.

Chapter 4

Economy

During the first half of the twentieth century, Korea endured one hardship after another. Japan began taking control of the Korean peninsula in 1905. In 1910, Japan formally annexed Korea and ruled the country for thirty-five years, and that rule aided Japan's economic development, not Korea's.

In 1945, the Allied victory in World War II ended Japan's occupation of Korea, but liberation and the beginning of the Cold War also split the peninsula into two countries and two very different economies. North Korea

▲ The Korean War left South Korea in a state of destruction and thousands of children orphaned. Even with foreign aid, the South Korean government was unable to repair the country and also care for the many parentless children then living on the streets.

had large manufacturing centers but little farming, while South Korea could feed itself but had little industry.

The new South Korean government had barely established itself before North Korea invaded in 1950, igniting the Korean War. The war ended in 1953, but three years of devastating conflict left South Korea in ruins. By the early 1960s, South Korea was one of the poorest countries in the world.

But South Korea pulled itself from the rubble. Through sheer determination and extraordinary leadership, the South Korean people rebuilt their country by creating manufacturing centers. Today, South Korea has a strong, stable economy, and South Koreans enjoy a high standard of living. Because of South Korea's rapid economic development, many people call South Korea an economic miracle.[1]

▶ Before the Miracle

During Japan's occupation of Korea, the Japanese held all the important jobs in government and industry and denied Koreans a good education. By the time South Korea had to govern itself, there were few people equipped to do so and no manufacturing base on which to build jobs or trade. When the peninsula was split, many people from the North fled South to escape the Communist regime. South Korea's farmland, which was already limited by the country's mountainous terrain, had been overworked by Japan and could not sustain all its people.

By the early 1960s, the South Korean economy was in terrible shape due to inflation, unemployment, and government corruption. Students demonstrated in the streets. On May 16, 1961, General Park Chung-hee and other military officers overthrew the South Korean government. General Park was elected president in 1963, but his presidency faced

▲ *Seoul is the capital of South Korea as well as the country's center for banking, commerce, and industry.*

overwhelming problems, since many South Koreans did not have jobs or even homes. The United States and other countries provided economic aid and military security to South Korea that helped it to survive this difficult period.

▶ How the Miracle Happened

President Park knew South Korea needed to start producing goods to trade to other countries. He devised a series of five-year plans to build industry and improve South Korea's economy. First he concentrated on restoring roads, power plants, schools, dams, homes, factories, and other structures that had been destroyed during the war. Then he focused on building new factories and centers where research and development could take place.

The government also began lending money to South Koreans who wanted to build certain kinds of businesses. South Korea's biggest resource was its millions of well-educated and hardworking people who would work for low wages, so these first businesses were light industries

29

The world's oldest rice grains, which may be as old as fifteen thousand years, were found by archaeologists in central South Korea. Today, South Koreans continue to cultivate this crop, which is the staple for more than half the world.

that needed many workers. South Korea imported raw materials. South Korean workers turned those materials into goods such as toys and fabric. South Korea then exported the finished goods.

As South Korea's economy grew, South Korean businesses expanded into heavy industry and technology. The country began producing chemicals, computer chips, electronics, automobiles, and ships. Today, South Korea exports products to countries all over the world. South Korean companies such as Samsung, which manufactures electronics such as televisions and stereos, and Hyundai, a carmaker, are known worldwide.

▶ The Chaebol

The South Korean government had a strong hand in each step of the country's economic development. For many years, the government set wages and fixed the prices of goods. It strictly controlled imports so that foreign-made products would not compete with South Korean products.

The government also granted special favors to certain businesses called chaebol. Chaebol are huge family-run corporations made up of many smaller companies. With help from the government, the chaebol grew and helped South Korea prosper. By the 1990s, the four largest chaebol accounted for nearly half of South Korea's economy. But because the chaebol could borrow money easily, they ran up large amounts of debt. Since the chaebol dominated South Korea's economy, smaller companies could not compete.

In 1997, the economies of some Asian countries, including South Korea, experienced a severe financial crisis. South Korean companies could not pay back their loans. Companies went bankrupt. South Korean workers lost their jobs. The *won,* South Korea's unit of currency, lost much of its value.

To become more profitable, the chaebol had to reform the way they did business. They could no longer rely on special favors from the government, and they could no longer run up huge debts. The South Korean government also reformed its banking system. These reforms helped the South Korean economy, and South Korea became one of the first countries to recover from Asia's economic crisis.

Agriculture

For centuries, Korea was a farming nation. South Korea still produces crops such as rice, ginseng, tea, barley, vegetables, and wheat. But over the past fifty years, as the country has become more industrialized, fewer and fewer young Koreans have taken up farming. More than 80 percent of Koreans now live in cities, and that number is expected to grow. Many of the people who raise crops today are older South Koreans who have farmed all their lives. They often farm by hand, using traditional methods rather than modern machinery.

Chapter 5

History

Since Korea lies between the Asian mainland and Japan, it has often been caught in power struggles between the countries that surround it. Through the centuries, China, the Mongols, Manchuria, Russia, and Japan have tried to control the Korean peninsula. After World War II, the Cold War conflict between the United States and the Soviet Union tore the peninsula in half.

But between periods of struggle were periods of peace. During these times, Korean culture flowered. Throughout history, art, language, culture, and ideas have flowed through Korea from Asia to Japan.

▶ The Three Kingdoms

The first kingdoms on the Korean peninsula emerged during Korea's Bronze Age (900–400 B.C.) The kingdom of Ko-Chosun, or Old Chosun, in the northern part of the peninsula, became the largest and strongest. It was so strong that it became a threat to China. The Chinese invaded and conquered Old Chosun in 108 B.C.

Soon three new Korean kingdoms emerged. Koguryo, a kingdom of fierce warriors, rose up in the northern part of the peninsula. Koguryo drove the Chinese out in A.D. 313. Warriors from Koguryo also captured lands in Manchuria, on the Asian mainland.

Another kingdom, Paekche, arose in the southwestern part of the peninsula. Paekche was peaceful and civilized. It developed trade with its neighbors and carried the culture and traditions of the Asian mainland to Japan.

The kingdom of Shilla rose up in the southeastern part of the peninsula. Shilla formed a military alliance with China. By A.D. 668, Shilla and its Chinese allies had conquered Paekche and Koguryo. China tried to take control of these conquered lands, but Shilla was able to drive the Chinese out. For the first time, the Korean peninsula was united under one rule.

For two centuries, Shilla was peaceful and prosperous. Buddhism, Confucianism, education, art, and culture flourished. Shilla kings built magnificent Buddhist temples. They developed an irrigation system for the rice fields and gave land to the poor.

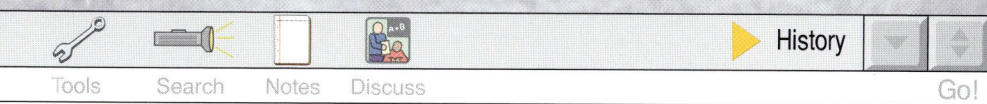

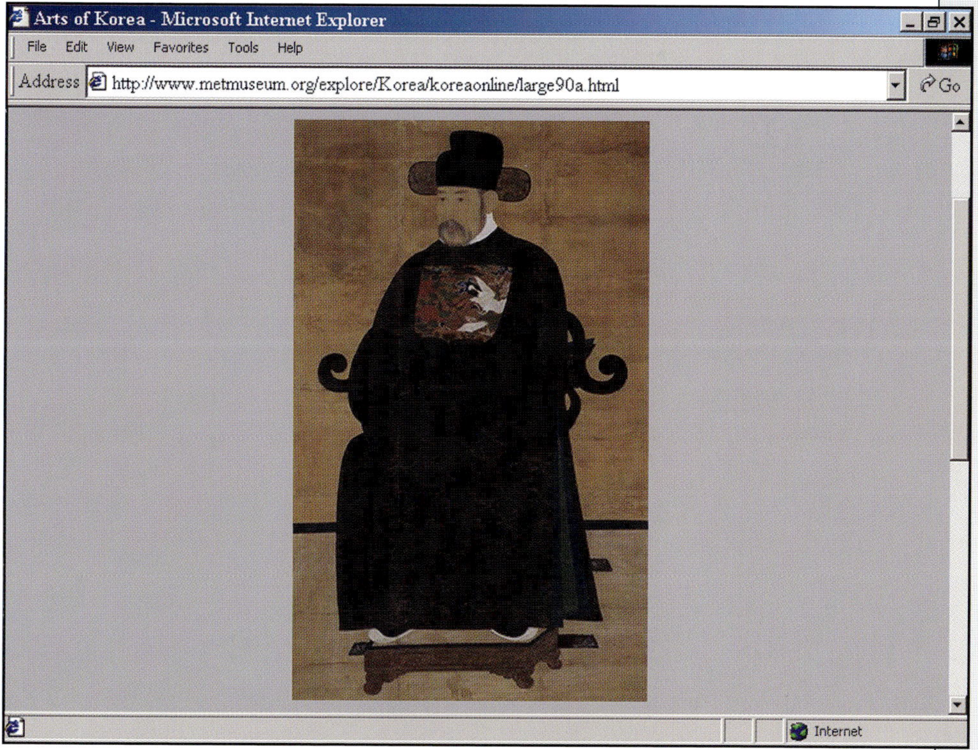

▲ *Korean portraits such as this one of Cho Mal-saeng (1370–1447), a Korean official, were painted to commemorate important occasions. In painting the portrait, the artist attempted to convey the subject's personality as well as show his or her appearance.*

Koryo

In the ninth century, Shilla's power crumbled. In 935, a general named Wang Kon conquered Shilla and established the kingdom called Koryo. The modern name *Korea* comes from the older name *Koryo*.

Once again, religion, art, and education flourished. Koreans began printing books using moveable type in the mid-1200s, two hundred years before Johannes Gutenberg invented the printing press in Europe. During the Koryo period, Koreans began producing the exquisite blue-green celadon pottery that they are still famous for.

Koryo fended off attacks from the Mongols and remained a stable kingdom for nearly five hundred years. But in the 1100s, conflicts arose between the government, the *yangban* (the noble class), the army, and Buddhist monks. Koryo's power declined. Japanese pirates and Chinese bandits raided the country. In 1259, the Mongols conquered Koryo.

Chosun

Koryo finally drove the Mongols out in 1356. But Koryo's government was not strong. A military officer, General Yi Song-gye, seized control of the peninsula in 1392. General Yi founded the Chosun dynasty, the line of kings that would rule until 1910.

Chosun kings governed according to the principles of Confucianism. Class structure was rigid, but art, education, and science flourished. King Sejong the Great, who ruled from 1418 to 1450, oversaw the creation of the Korean alphabet, hangul. During Sejong's rule, Koreans also developed a rain gauge, instruments to measure wind speed and direction, sundials, astronomical maps, observatories, and clocks.

Turtle Ships

In 1592, Japan invaded Chosun. Japan wanted to use the peninsula to stage attacks on China. The Japanese army, much stronger than Chosun's army, soon overran the Korean peninsula.

But Chosun's navy was powerful. Admiral Yi Sunsin commanded a fleet of ships on the peninsula's southern coast. Admiral Yi covered some of his wooden vessels with iron plates, creating the world's first ironclad ships. These iron plates repelled Japanese cannonballs and fire-tipped arrows. The iron covering resembled a turtle's shell, and Koreans called these ships "turtle ships." The turtle ships sank hundreds of Japanese ships. Admiral Yi's fleet cut off Japanese supply lines and prevented Japanese soldiers from landing on the peninsula.

The Hermit Kingdom

The Koreans finally drove the Japanese out in 1598, but fighting had destroyed much of the farmland. The Japanese also captured

Sunjong was the last emperor of Korea. His rule began in 1907 and came to an end when Korea was formally annexed by Japan in 1910.

35

many of Chosun's artists and scientists and took them to Japan. In the early 1600s, Manchuria attacked, and Chosun was forced to accept the Manchu Empire as a superior nation.

Chosun was tired of fighting. Its leaders wanted to protect and rebuild Chosun. They isolated the peninsula from the world. Chosun closed its borders to all foreigners except the Chinese. It outlawed Christianity, a western religion. Chosun became known as the "Hermit Kingdom." By the late 1800s, Korea began opening its doors to the West when it signed trade agreements with the United States and other countries.

▶ A Japanese Colony

But Korea was still caught in struggles between its neighbors. Japan, China, and Russia each wanted to control Korea. In 1895, Japan defeated China in the Sino-Japanese War. In 1905, Japan defeated Russia in the Russo-Japanese War. Then Japan began taking control of the Korean peninsula. In 1905, Japan forced Korea to accept a Protectorate Treaty. This treaty allowed Japan to control Korea's foreign relations, police, army, and banks. In 1910, Japan formally annexed Korea.

For the next thirty-five years, Japan ruled Korea as a colony, and Japan's rule of Korea was harsh. The Japanese outlawed the Korean language. They forced Koreans to adopt Japanese surnames and to worship at Japanese Shinto shrines. They ordered Korean men to cut their hair so that they could no longer wear their traditional Confucian topknot. They replaced the books in Korean schools with books written in Japanese and refused to allow Korean students to learn Korean history. They took half of Korea's rice crop. When World War II broke out,

Japan forced some Korean men to fight in the Japanese army and others to work in Japanese airplane factories and ammunition plants.

▶ Two Koreas

In 1945, the Allies, which included the United States and the Soviet Union, defeated the Axis powers, which included Japan, in World War II. The Allies forced Japan out of Korea, but the now-liberated Korea was divided into North Korea, administered by the Soviet Union, and South Korea, administered by the United States. That division, proposed as a temporary solution to ease Korea back into independence, still exists.

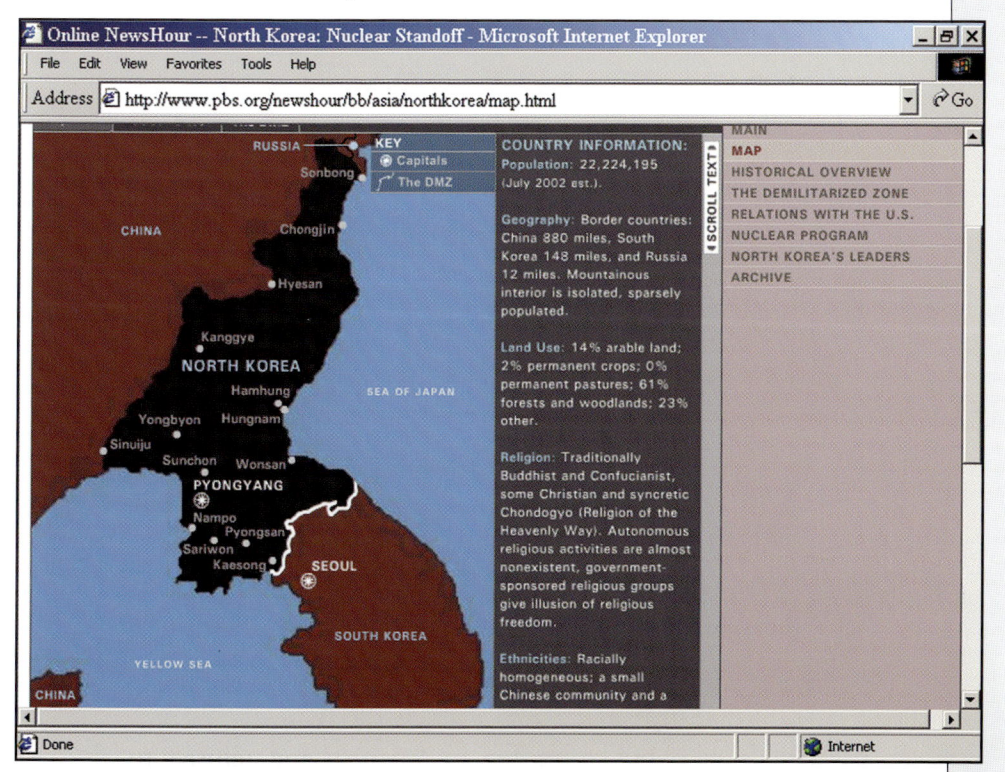

▲ Socialist and nationalist groups in Korea formed in opposition to Japanese occupation of the peninsula. After World War II, these groups would rule North Korea.

The United States, the Soviet Union, and other countries could not agree on how Korea should be governed. The newly formed United Nations tried to set up elections so that Korea could determine its own fate, but the Soviet Union prevented elections in North Korea. South Korea did hold elections in May 1948, electing representatives to its National Assembly. The National Assembly drafted a constitution, named South Korea the Republic of Korea, and in July elected Yi Sung-man, more commonly known as Syngman Rhee, as the republic's first president. On August 15, exactly three years after Korea had been liberated from the Japanese, the Republic of Korea declared itself a sovereign state. On September 9, the Soviet Union established a Communist government in North Korea.

The Korean War and Aftermath

On June 25, 1950, North Korea invaded South Korea. Troops from the United States and sixteen other United Nations countries came to the aid of South Korea. War raged for three years. The Soviet Union and China reinforced North Korea with troops and supplies. In 1953, the two sides finally reached an agreement that

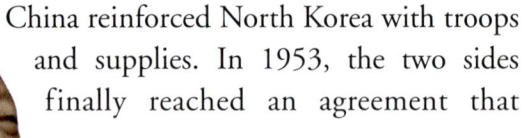

◀ *Syngman Rhee*

Kim Dae-jung – Biography

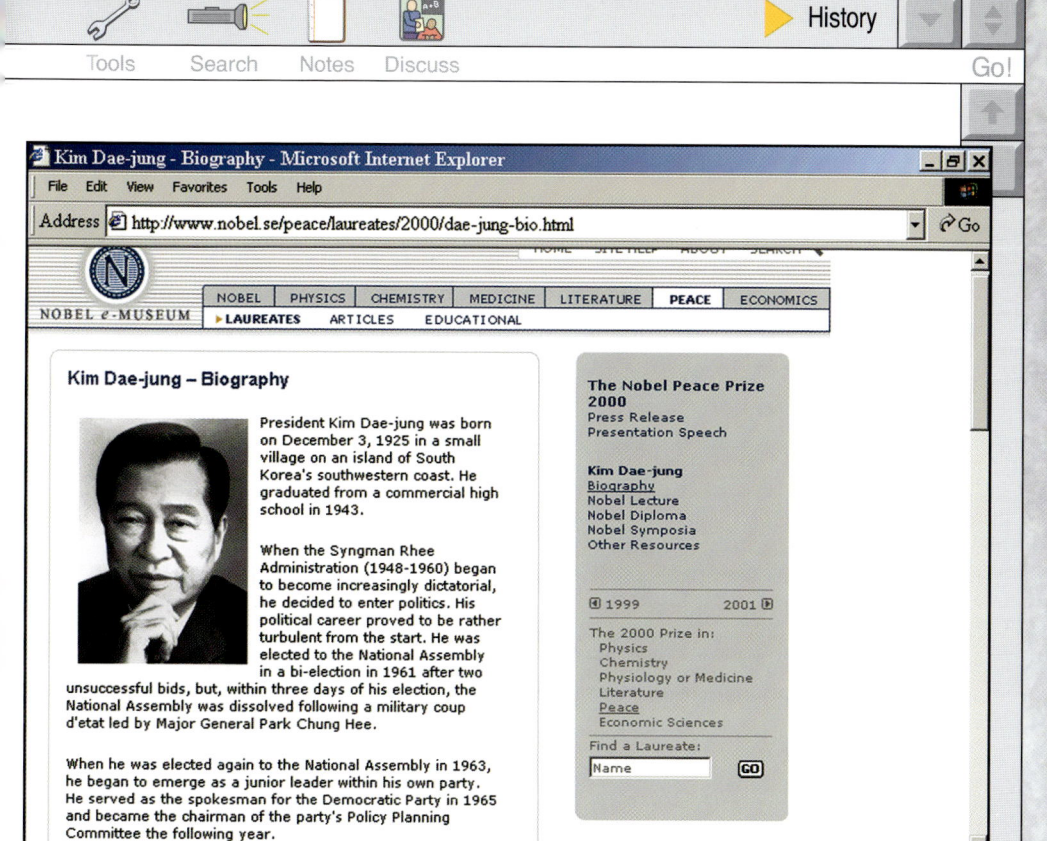

President Kim Dae-jung was born on December 3, 1925 in a small village on an island of South Korea's southwestern coast. He graduated from a commercial high school in 1943.

When the Syngman Rhee Administration (1948-1960) began to become increasingly dictatorial, he decided to enter politics. His political career proved to be rather turbulent from the start. He was elected to the National Assembly in a bi-election in 1961 after two unsuccessful bids, but, within three days of his election, the National Assembly was dissolved following a military coup d'etat led by Major General Park Chung Hee.

When he was elected again to the National Assembly in 1963, he began to emerge as a junior leader within his own party. He served as the spokesman for the Democratic Party in 1965 and became the chairman of the party's Policy Planning Committee the following year.

▲ Kim Dae-jung spent many years fighting for democracy in South Korea before he was elected president in December 1997.

ended the fighting in the Korean War, although a peace agreement was never signed.

The fighting devastated the peninsula. Millions of South Koreans were killed or wounded, and millions more were left homeless. Syngman Rhee's government stayed in power throughout the 1950s but was weak and corrupt. Students staged protests, asking for government reforms. Finally, in 1960, President Rhee resigned.

South Korea's new president, Yun Po-sun, and prime minister, Chang Myon, could not control the unrest in the country. In 1961, General Park Chung-hee overthrew the government, beginning a thirty-one-year period of military rule in South Korea. In 1963, he resigned from the army and was elected president. President Park governed with a strong hand, and his government became more and more repressive, but he was able to pull South Korea's economy from ruin. He was reelected in 1967 and 1971. The president's wife was killed in 1974 during an assassination attempt meant for him. He served as South Korea's president until 1979, when he was assassinated by the head of South Korea's intelligence agency.

For most of the 1980s, military dictators controlled South Korea. Chun Doo-hwan, a major general in the South Korean army, succeeded Park as president in 1981, but he left office voluntarily in 1987, as South Korean students and others demanded a democratic government.

Since 1987, when South Korea elected Roh Tae-woo, it has elected presidents to single five-year terms. Although Roh was democratically elected, Koreans considered him to be the last leader of the military governments, since he was a soldier for most of his life.

Finally, in 1993, South Koreans elected Kim Young Sam, the country's first real civilian president. In 1997, Kim Dae-jung was the first leader of an opposition party to be elected president. He began a "sunshine policy" to try to repair the relationship between North and South Korea. In 2000, he became the first South Korean president to visit North Korea. That year, Kim Dae-jung was awarded the Nobel Peace Prize "for his work for democracy and human rights in South Korea and in East Asia in general, and for peace and reconciliation with North Korea in particular."[1]

Chapter 6 ▶

Korean Americans

Korean Americans are one of the fastest growing immigrant groups in the United States. Korean-American families value education, and Korean-American children typically do well in school. Korean Americans graduate from high school and earn college degrees in higher numbers than Americans on average.[1]

But Korean Americans sometimes feel invisible. Other Americans often lump Korean Americans together with other Asian Americans.

▶ Early Korean Immigrants

During the late 1800s, a handful of Korean immigrants trickled into the United States. Some of these immigrants were traders or farmworkers. Some, such as Philip Jaisohn, were political exiles. In 1880, Philip Jaisohn was the first Korean to become an American citizen. In 1882, he was the first Korean American to earn a medical degree in the United States.

But the first large group of Koreans did not begin to immigrate to the United States until 1903. On January 13 of that year, a ship carrying about one hundred Koreans docked in Hawaii. Over the next two years, seven thousand more Koreans moved to Hawaii to work on sugar plantations. Plantation owners had promised good pay and free housing. But plantation work was harsh. Korean workers toiled ten hours a day, six days a week. They lived in wretched shacks and earned less than one dollar per day. Many Korean workers left the plantations to find work in

Hawaiian cities. Others left to seek jobs on the mainland of the United States.

In 1905, two years after the first Korean plantation workers arrived in Hawaii, Japan began taking over Korea. The Japanese rulers refused to allow Koreans to leave Korea.

▶ Picture Brides

Japan did make one exception. Most of the Korean immigrants to America were men, and they wanted to marry Korean women. The men mailed photographs of themselves to matchmakers in Korea. If a Korean woman liked a man's picture, she would mail a photo of herself back to him. If the man liked the woman's picture, too, they would make

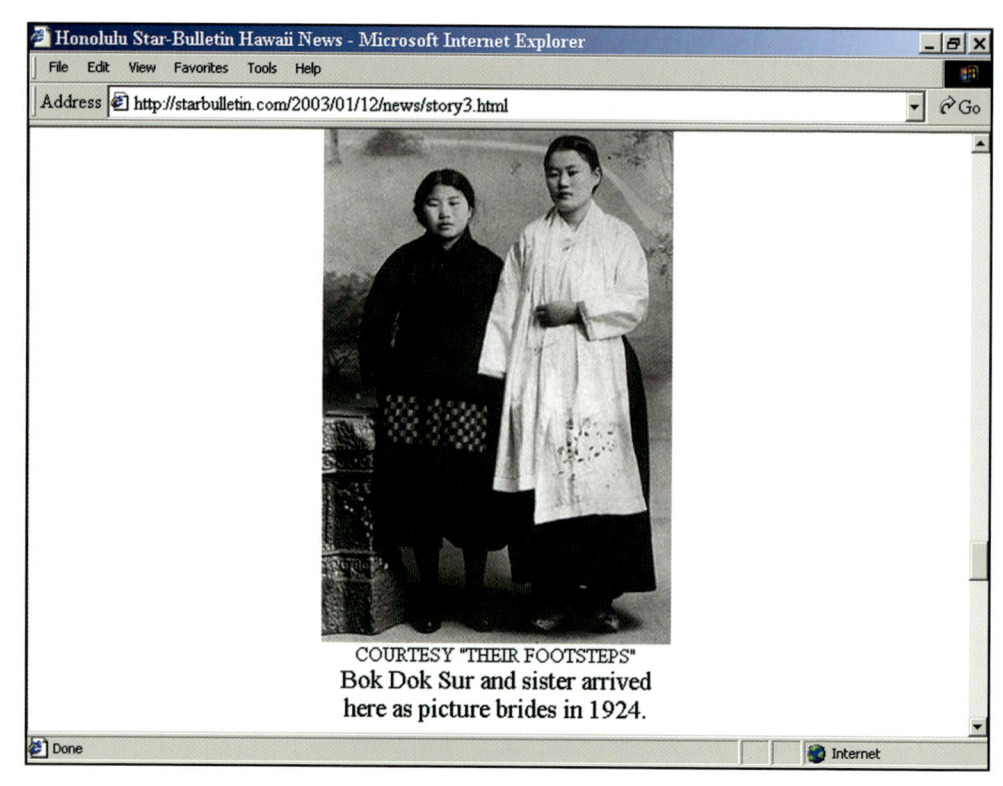

COURTESY "THEIR FOOTSTEPS"
Bok Dok Sur and sister arrived here as picture brides in 1924.

▲ *Korean picture brides were mostly between the ages of seventeen and twenty, usually a whole generation younger than their husbands.*

42

arrangements for marriage. The woman, called a picture bride, would sail to America. The man and woman would marry as soon as the woman arrived, before she even left the ship. The Japanese allowed about a thousand Korean picture brides to immigrate to the United States.

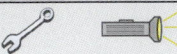

▶ Discrimination in the New Land

Koreans and other Asian immigrants faced discrimination in their new country. Many other Americans were suspicious of people whose traditions and culture were so different from their own. They were afraid Asian Americans would take their jobs. California passed laws banning Korean-American children from attending schools. They prevented Korean Americans from owning property. In 1924, the United States passed the Oriental Exclusion Act. This law banned Asians from immigrating to America for three decades.

▶ Later Immigrants

During the early 1950s, many American soldiers fighting in the Korean War married Korean women. Since these wives and children were dependents of American citizens, they could legally come to the United States. In addition, American families adopted about one hundred fifty thousand Korean children who had been orphaned by the war. In 1952, the United States changed its immigration laws. The new laws allowed one hundred Koreans each year to immigrate to America.

Thirteen years later, the United States passed the 1965 Immigration and Nationality Act. This law allowed more people to immigrate. South Koreans began streaming to America to escape poverty and crowded South Korean cities. Today, there are more than one million Americans of Korean ancestry who live in the United States.[2]

Paik studied music composition first in Korea, then at the University of Tokyo, where he wrote his thesis on Modernist composer Arnold Schoenberg. In 1956 Paik traveled to Europe and settled in Germany to pursue his interest in avant-garde music and performance. During studies at the Summer Course for New Music in Darmstaat in 1958, he met composer John Cage. Cage's ideas on composition and performance were a great influence on Paik, as

Nam June Paik, 1986. Photo by Rainer Rosenow.

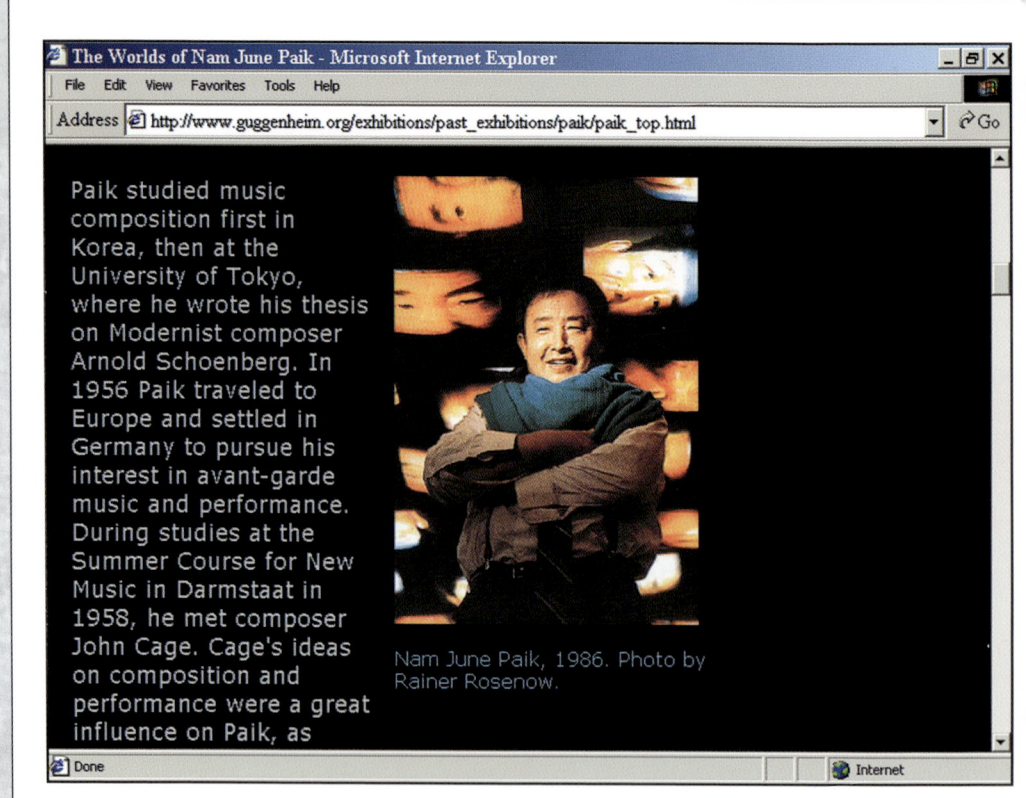

▲ Nam June Paik, a native of South Korea, pioneered the use in art of electronic moving images transmitted by television, video, and lasers.

▶ **Life in America**

The 1965 law gave preference to immigrants who were highly skilled or were relatives of American citizens. In the 1960s and 1970s, many Korean doctors and nurses came to the United States. They settled in large cities that had a shortage of medical professionals. Scientists and those with technology skills soon followed. Large Korean-American communities grew up in Los Angeles and New York City. Koreatown, in Los Angeles, became a thriving Korean-American community.

Today many Korean Americans own their own small businesses, such as shops, restaurants, and dry cleaners. Many Korean Americans own fruit and vegetable stores.

Famous Korean Americans

Korean Americans have succeeded in many professions, including the arts. Writer Younghill Kang moved to the United States from Korea in 1921. He began his writing career in 1931. His first novel, *The Grass Roof*, is about a young man in Korea. Writer Linda Sue Park's parents were Korean immigrants. Park won the Newbery Medal in 2002 for her novel *A Single Shard*. It tells the story of an orphan boy who becomes an apprentice potter in twelfth-century Korea.

Artist Nam June Paik was born in Seoul, Korea, in 1932. He left during the Korean War and eventually settled in New York. His multimedia works, which use television screens and other high-tech equipment, have been exhibited in galleries and museums around the world.

Korean-American women have taken the golfing world by storm. At age ten, Korean American Michelle Wie became the youngest golfer to ever qualify for a United States Golf Association amateur tournament. In 2002, twelve-year-old Wie became the youngest player to qualify for a Ladies Professional Golf Association (LPGA) tournament. In 2004, fourteen-year-old Wie played in the Sony Open, a men's PGA event. Se Ri Pak was the LPGA Rookie of the Year in 1998. She became the youngest player to win the U.S. Women's Open golf tournament. She was born in Daejeon, South Korea, and now lives in Florida.

Many Korean Americans believe in the Confucian ideals of education, duty, and hard work that their ancestors were raised to believe in. Those beliefs helped their ancestors raise South Korea from the rubble of the Korean War and continue to sustain Korean Americans as they work to succeed in their new lives in the United States.

Chapter Notes

South Korea Facts

1. The *World Factbook 2003*, "South Korea," August 1, 2003, <http://www.cia.gov/cia/publications/factbook/print/ks.html> (October 19, 2003).

2. Ibid.

3. Ibid.

Chapter 1. Korea: Land of the Morning Calm

1. Tom Le Bas, *Insight Guides Korea* (London: Langenscheidt Publishers, 2002), p. 15.

2. Joe Havely, "Korea's DMZ: 'Scariest Place on Earth,'" CNN.com/World, February 20, 2002, <http://www.cnn.com/2002/WORLD/asiapcf/east/02/19/koreas.dmz/> (October 19, 2003).

Chapter 2. Land and Climate

1. S. E. Solberg, *The Land and People of Korea* (New York: HarperCollins Publishers, 1991), p. 11.

2. Tom O'Neill, "DMZ—Korea's Dangerous Divide," *National Geographic* magazine, July 2003, p. 26.

Chapter 3. Culture

1. The *World Factbook 2003*, "South Korea," August 1, 2003, <http://www.cia.gov/cia/publications/factbook/print/ks.html> (October 19, 2003).

Chapter 4. Economy

1. James Hoare and Susan Pares, *Korea: An Introduction* (London: Kegan Paul International, 1988), p. 91.

Chapter 5. History

1. "The Nobel Peace Prize 2000," Nobel e-Museum, October 13, 2000, <http://www.nobel.se/peace/laureates/2000/press.html> (October 20, 2003).

Chapter 6. Korean Americans

1. *We, the Americans: Asians*, U.S. Department of Commerce, Bureau of the Census (Washington, D.C.: September 1993), p. 4.

2. Jessica S. Barnes and Claudette E. Bennett, *The Asian Population: 2000*, U.S. Department of Commerce, Bureau of the Census (Washington, D.C.: February 2002), p. 9.

Further Reading

Collinwood, Dean. *Korea: The High and Beautiful Peninsula.* New York: Marshall Cavendish, 1997.

Connor, Mary E. *The Koreas: A Global Studies Handbook.* Santa Barbara, Calif.: ABC CLIO, 2002.

Farley, Carol. *Korea: Land of the Morning Calm.* New York: Dillon Press, 1999.

Hill, Valerie. *Korea.* Broomall, Pa.: Mason Crest Publishers, 2003.

Lehrer, Brian. *The Korean Americans.* Broomall, Pa.: Chelsea House, 1996.

Masse, Johanna. *South Korea.* Milwaukee: Gareth Stevens Publishing, 2002.

McNair, Sylvia. *Korea.* Chicago: Children's Press, 1986.

Salter, Christopher L. *South Korea.* Broomall, Pa.: Chelsea House, 2003.

Schlesinger, Arthur M., Jr., ed. *Kim Dae Jung: South Korean President.* Broomall, Pa.: Chelsea House, 1999.

Shepheard, Patricia. *South Korea.* Broomall, Pa.: Chelsea House, 1999.

Stickler, John. *Land of Morning Calm: Korean Culture Then and Now.* Fremont, Calif.: Shen's Books, 2003.

Young, Jeff C. *The Korean War: A MyReportLinks.com Book.* Berkeley Heights, N.J.: Enslow Publishers, Inc., 2003.

Index

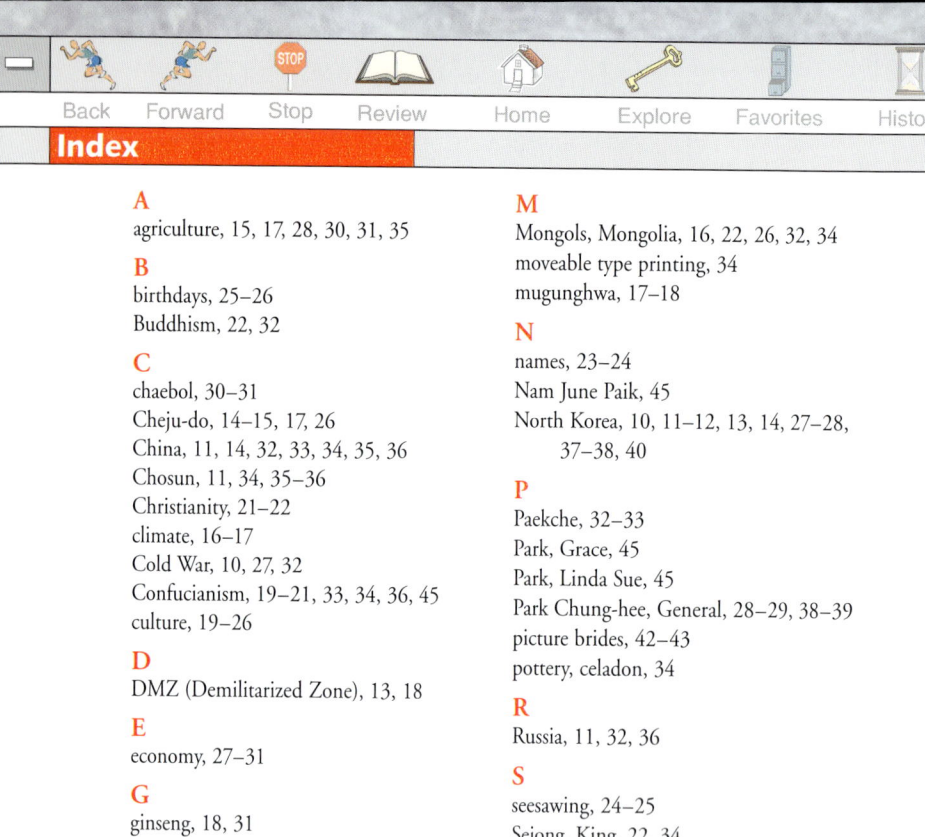

A
agriculture, 15, 17, 28, 30, 31, 35

B
birthdays, 25–26
Buddhism, 22, 32

C
chaebol, 30–31
Cheju-do, 14–15, 17, 26
China, 11, 14, 32, 33, 34, 35, 36
Chosun, 11, 34, 35–36
Christianity, 21–22
climate, 16–17
Cold War, 10, 27, 32
Confucianism, 19–21, 33, 34, 36, 45
culture, 19–26

D
DMZ (Demilitarized Zone), 13, 18

E
economy, 27–31

G
ginseng, 18, 31
Gobi Desert, 18

H
Halla-san, 9, 14–15
hanbok, 19
hangul (Korean alphabet), 22–23, 34
harabang, 26
history, 11–13, 32–40
hwangsa, 17

J
Jaisohn, Philip, 41
Japan, 11, 14, 27, 28, 32, 34, 35, 37, 38, 42–43

K
Kim Dae-jung, 39, 40
Kim Young Sam, 40
kimchi, 19, 20
Ko-Chosun (Old Chosun), 32
Koguryo, 32–33
Korean Americans, 41–45
Korean War, 12, 13, 17, 27, 28, 38, 43
Koryo, 34

L
land and climate, 14–18
language, 22–23, 36

M
Mongols, Mongolia, 16, 22, 26, 32, 34
moveable type printing, 34
mugunghwa, 17–18

N
names, 23–24
Nam June Paik, 45
North Korea, 10, 11–12, 13, 14, 27–28, 37–38, 40

P
Paekche, 32–33
Park, Grace, 45
Park, Linda Sue, 45
Park Chung-hee, General, 28–29, 38–39
picture brides, 42–43
pottery, celadon, 34

R
Russia, 11, 32, 36

S
seesawing, 24–25
Sejong, King, 22, 34
Seoul, 9, 15, 19, 29, 45
shamanism, 22
Shilla, 33, 34
Soviet Union, 11–12, 13, 32, 37–38
sports, 24–25
Syngman Rhee, 38

T
Taegeuk-gi (South Korea's flag), 9
Tan'gun, 10–11
turtle ships, 35

U
United States, 11–12, 13, 16, 29, 32, 36, 37–38, 41–45

W
Wie, Michelle, 45
won, 9, 31
World War II, 11, 27, 32, 36–37

Y
yangban, 34
Yellow Sea, 14, 15–16
Yi Song-gye, General, 34
Yi Sunsin, Admiral, 35
Younghill Kang, 45

FEB 2 3 2009
2526